De

Many thanks for your support. May God continue to bless you, and yours.

Sincerely
"Lillian Keith Davis"
2006

"I Won't Be Denied"

By

Lillian Keith Lewis

1663 LIBERTY DRIVE, SUITE 200
BLOOMINGTON, INDIANA 47403
(800) 839-8640
WWW.AUTHORHOUSE.COM

© *2005 Lillian Keith Lewis. All Rights Reserved.*

No part of this book may be reproduced, stored in a retrieval system, or transmitted by any means without the written permission of the author.

First published by AuthorHouse 01/18/05

ISBN: 1-4184-6357-4 (e)
ISBN: 1-4184-3435-3 (sc)

Printed in the United States of America
Bloomington, Indiana

This book is printed on acid-free paper.

"I Won't Be Denied"

Isn't it amazing how the mind absorbs and projects the incidents of life? I remember a cold winter day in Atlanta, Georgia at my great aunt's home (Aunt Ellen) we had just finished a hot breakfast of hot biscuits, jelly, butter, streak-a-lean bacon and eggs and coffee for the grown ups when my mother's father showed up unexpectedly. That was the first and last time I saw my grandfather. I was in awe of him because he was a tall, dark, handsome man that spoke in a mild mannered voice that made you want him to keep talking. I remember thinking wouldn't it be fun to have my grandfather around me all of the time, but that wasn't to be because just like he appeared he left the same way going back to Chattanooga where he lived.

You see my mother and father met fell in love in Atlanta where I was conceived, then they moved to Chattanooga where I was born. When I was a toddler, they moved back to Atlanta where my brother was born. He was so pretty, curly headed light brown skin little boy. His name was Roy after my father's brother whom I adored; I always called my brother "Little Brother" so the nickname stuck.

Times were really hard, and money was very scarce. My uncle got a job for my dad in Chattanooga (my hometown) and we moved back where we stayed. My mother found a job doing domestic work. Back then people rented rooms with the use of the kitchen and bathroom. My mother was a tall, reddish brown-skinned, full bosom woman, with beautiful light brown eyes and a head full of beautiful hair. She was a vision of loveliness, but there was always sadness about her. She lost her mother at the age of fourteen years old after which she was thrown from place to place with relatives that weren't very nice to her.

After she and my father moved back to Chattanooga she was disappointed in love because of him being young and "sowing his wild oats" as the old folks use to say. When my mother went to work, my dad would come home at lunchtime, sometimes bringing the woman he went with along and would make us go outside to play (me and my little brother). Even then, I had sense enough to know this was wrong.

The lady where we stayed, I'll call her Mrs. Ann, would sneak and tell my mother what had gone on while she was at work. It would hurt her deeply, but she never said anything, until one day she just got fed up and called her step-brother (Uncle James). He told her to get a cab and come out to stay with the rest of the family until she could get on her feet and he would help her all he could.

Two or three nights before we left my dad, I had ten pennies laying on the dresser that had been given to me and I was excited about what I was going to buy with them. Back then you could buy quite a bit of treats with ten pennies. I went to bed happy, but woke up to see my pennies gone. I knew right away, what had happened to my little treasure. My temper flared.

My mother took me by the hand and said; "Don't say anything about the pennies being gone because it would cause problems."

I had to keep my mouth closed even though I was upset, but even back then I vowed "I won't be denied." When I get grown I'm going to let them know how I feel. For some reason, the time as yet has not presented itself.

Well, Mrs. Ann came back with more news and my mother began to get very tired of this carrying on behind her back. She began to take on extra work of washing and ironing to save money so we would have enough to carry us over after moving. In the meantime, Mrs. Ann's brother-in-law and his wife stayed upstairs. He was tall, thin, and good-looking with nice hair. His wife, who I'll call Aunt Doe, was mixed and simply beautiful; her father was white and mother black. All of the kids in the neighborhood dearly loved her because she was a caring, sharing individual, but Uncle Lee was a sneaky, dirty-minded person who would give us candy not to tell that he was feeling on the private parts of the little girls eleven and up that came over to play with Mrs. Ann's nieces.

One day we went upstairs and asked Uncle Lee for some candy. He told us we couldn't come in because Aunt Doe was gone to work. He hurried and gave us the candy and told us to go back out to play.

Just as we started down the steps, a familiar voice said, "Are they gone Uncle Lee?"

He answered, "Yeah, they gone", but we weren't; we stayed quiet because we knew she would have to come out to go home, and when she did we would see her.

Sure enough, out she came and when she saw us sitting on the steps, she got mad and yelled at us. We yelled back at her saying, "We going to tell your mama, we going to tell your mama."

Of course, she didn't want that so she buttered us up with more candy and by the time Mrs. Ann came out of the kitchen where she was cooking dinner to see what all of the noise was about, the girl had bribed us with candy and sweet words.

Finally, one day Aunt Doe returned home early and caught Uncle Lee doing his usual sneaky, lowdown tactics. They had a terrible fight and the next day when Uncle Lee went to work, beautiful Aunt Doe kissed us all good bye called a yellow cab and was gone. Uncle Lee went down like a piece of concrete in the river. He never did find out where she went.

I think this gave my mother the courage to make a move and start a new life. The next time my dad stayed out all night, my mother got me and my brother up, bathed us, combed my hair, helped us to dress (she had packed our clothes while we slept), got dressed herself, called uncle James (her brother) to come and get us, which he did. But it seems that all of the hurt that she had endured surfaced, she tore the sheets and pillowcases and piled them up in the floor, knocked the chimney out of the wall, took the soot after piling his clothes up in the floor, and spread it all over them--and away we went to live with our relatives.

We were told that my dad came home shortly after we left. When he walked in and saw the mess that had been left for him, he ran out like a madman wanting to know where we had gone, but Mrs. Ann could only tell him a man came to pick us up because she had never met my uncle James.

Everyone was so nice to us. My mother got a better job. She met a nice man that truly cared for her and was good to my little brother and me. Life was sweet until one day I was coming out of the store; I looked and saw my dad walking up the road. All of the streets were not paved at that time. I started running as fast as I could to tell my mother he had found us.

She calmly came to the door as he walked toward us smiling saying I'm not going to hurt you. I just want to talk to you. My mother stood her ground not moving an inch holding me by the hand. My little brother was inside taking a nap. She never said much

"I Won't Be Denied"

except to say no, no more talking I'm through with you. She turned carrying me with her went inside, closed the door and left him standing outside. Finally, he walked away.

After that I made new friends; we played, picked wild greens, blackberries and looked forward to getting dressed up to go to Sunday School and church. I loved the beautiful music and singing! I didn't realize how important the preaching was; I just wanted the good Reverend to hurry so I could enjoy the beautiful music and singing again. It was a joy to learn the Easter speeches and show off our new clothes.

There were other special days we looked forward to with great Joy. May Day, 4th July, Thanksgiving, Christmas, birthdays, of course first day, and last day of school because you got new clothes and shoes. Saturday night was a special night at our house because my great- uncle would invite three of his friends over to play a little music. One played the rub board, one turned a tub upside down and beat it, and one played the juice harp.

I loved dancing and could really dance! They would start around 8:00 and play until 11:00 - 12:00.

My great-aunt and my mother would fry fish and we would have an eating good time. My great-uncle and his buddies would enjoy corn squeezing. My great-aunt thought I didn't know, but I knew she was hitting the corn squeezing too, because she was awful happy. She had long legs, and would grab the tail of her dress, and I'm here to tell you, the high steppers didn't have a thing on her! She could do some great dancing that they called sets.

It was a sad day when my great-uncle passed. I was afraid to look at him. During those days, they would bring the bodies' home and family and friends would sit up all night until it was time to go to the funeral. I breathed a sigh of relief when they took the body from the house. For days, I wouldn't go in the front room where he was. I was sorry he had passed and I knew we would really miss him, but on the other hand, it was a relief.

Sometimes when my mother was at work I would sit and think about the things that were happening around me and how much I wanted my mother to approve of me. I wondered how it would feel for her to say, "I love you baby." I knew she loved me and was always good to me, but she just seemed to have a hard time expressing that love in the way I wanted her to. So to get her approval I always tried to do everything to please her so she would smile that beautiful way only she could do.

I was taught to pray early in life and knew the power of prayer because God had taken good care of us. Terror struck my heart on the day Little brother and I crossed the street with a group of our playmates. I tried to get to him but I was too late. A car hit him, dragging him almost a block.

I remember running to tell my mother. She began to scream and scream. I felt so helpless. Jesus, if I could ease the pain that she was going through! She tried so hard to make things easy for us. Well my mother never got over my little brothers death or my uncles, but life goes on.

This nice man she had met was real nice to us, and loved my mother dearly. They began to make plans to get married and we all were excited and happy about the upcoming event, but the day (Friday) before Mommie and Mr. Nice were to marry, he had a heart attack and died on the job. I thought, Jesus how many more disappointments can Mommie stand? She was so sad!

His family was very nice to Mommie and me. They wanted her to have everything that he had left except for some keepsakes to remember him by. Things were slow moving and it seemed like we would never get back to normal. Finally, we were up and back into the mainstream again.

Well, it's almost time to go back to school and all of the kids in the neighborhood are excited because that means new clothes, and seeing everyone we hadn't seen all summer and swapping stories about where we'd been and what we had done for the summer.

The first day of school is finally here and I'm out of bed like a shot. My pretty clothes had been laid out the night before. I was so anxious to get dressed and go out to join my friends.

Mommie came into the room and said, "Well young lady, this is your big dress up day. Come now and get your teeth brushed; your bath is ready in the middle room."

So away I went to get ready. I brushed my teeth with baking soda and salt rinsed my mouth out with

"I Won't Be Denied"

warm water, stuck my toes into the tin tub and out again because the water was too hot, so I just sat in the cane bottom chair and waited for it to cool enough for me to bath. I reached for the octagon soap and my washrag. I began to feel anxious again so, I began to soap my body down with the octagon soap after washing my face. I rinsed off good, stepped out, and dried off with the big homemade towel, reached for the (blue seal) Vaseline and Jergens lotion. By that time, my face felt as tight as a drum. So, I rubbed a lot of lotion on my face and arms. I used the Vaseline on my legs and feet. Then it was time to put on my Sunday underclothes.

Mommie took the brown paper curlers out of my hair so she could arrange my hair after I finished my breakfast of hoecake bread and cheese and milk. Of course, I hurriedly finished breakfast. Time was wasting and it was time to finish getting ready.

I felt great as I put my pretty white socks, black patent Sunday shoes, and at last, my beautiful blue and white organdy dress with the beautiful white satin sash. My Mommie tied the beautiful bow in the back and last but not least, the beautiful bow in the top of my curls. Oh my I felt like a princess and was out of the door in a flash.

I ran as fast as I could by Mommie to join my friends who were dressed up too. We were all smiles, chatting without ceasing. They were admiring my Shirley Temple curls. They were really pretty; oh, I felt great as I walked into the classroom and spoke to my teacher. She was a beautiful, brown-skinned woman that truly loved all of the kids she taught.

Well, all too soon, it was time to go home to do our chores of bringing the water and wood in for the next day. You see the water was outside. After we finished, our chores we put on our old play clothes and began to go over the events of the first day of school.

Well, it's time for me to go inside for supper and I'm really ready for it. Green beans with potatoes on top, fried okra, boiled okra, sliced tomatoes and onions, corn bread, fried chicken, apple cobbler, and lemonade.

"Gang way so I can wash my hands! I'm starving!"

Dinner is over and everyone is full and happy, except me, and I would be if Aunt Sadie wouldn't say

"I Won't Be Denied"

after we finished eating, "Thank the Lord, Bless the cook and I don't care who wash the dishes."

That meant I would wash the dishes and I hated for her to say that! Oh well, I better get the dishes washed and kitchen floor swept so I can go listen to the radio before bedtime. Mommie's calling me from the kitchen where she's slicing streak-a-lean bacon for tomorrow's breakfast.

I walked to the door and said, "Yes Mommie?"

She looked up from slicing bacon and said smiling, "You've had a busy day, aren't you tired?"

"A little", I said while yawning at the same time.

"Get ready for bed and don't forget to say your prayers."

After getting my pj's, saying my prayers, "Now I lay me down to sleep, I pray thee Lord my soul to keep, if I should die before I wake I pray the Lord my soul to take, bless Mommie, Daddy, all of my family and friends, even my teachers and principal and also the truant officer, Mr. Richardson" that we were all deathly afraid of. Oh well, I'm getting real sleepy and Mommie is getting ready for bed.

As I watched her by the lamplight, my mind went back to a time when Mommie had to work long hours and there was no one to keep Little Brother and me. My dad wasn't with us for some reason or other, but Mommie talked with a lady that ran an orphan home and she put me and little brother there and got a room across the street to be near us. Later every evening she would come over and bath us, talk to us and tuck us in and then help the lady that ran the orphan home get the other children ready for bed. It worked out fine.

She would leave us with tears rolling down her face with a promise that we would be together all of the time. After she got home (across the street), she would sit in the window looking toward the building where we were. I imagine she was crying and praying for things to get better and eventually they did.

One day we were outside playing in the swings and it was my time to push the person in the swing. Just as I pushed her, someone called me and I turned to answer and got hit by the swing. I'm now wearing that scar by my eye today. It hurt like everything!

"I Won't Be Denied"

I remember crying, "I want my Mommie. Am I gonna die?" I was scared and when Mommie saw me she was really upset, and made hurried plans to get a place where we could be together.

Gee, I'm sleepy. I'd better go to sleep so I can get up and get dressed in new navy blue dress trimmed in white ric-rac, put my blue bow in my Shirley Temple curls, and wear my favorite white roman sandals.

"Goodnight Mommie, goodnight, sleep tight; don't let the bedbugs bite." As I giggled, I scooted over close to Mommie and went to sleep.

The next morning was pretty much like the first day of school. We really enjoyed walking and talking to each other, full of plans, and excited about everything. As we entered the classroom, our teacher was standing at the end of the black board where she had written questions and left blank spaces for us to fill in. I was anxious to get busy so I could try for a good grade to show Mommie so she would be proud of me.

You see, education was very important to her because she had to quit school to work. That's why she wanted me to be able to finish school and to learn as much as I could while I was going. I would pray real hard asking God to help me be able to pass in all of my lessons. He always answered my prayers!

There was a lot of activity going on in our neighborhood. We had two friends that lived in our neighborhood that never got a chance to come outside in the yard to play with us. Their parents ran a store and they stayed in the back, but we were never allowed to go inside except to buy something. These kids were pitiful. It was a lonely life they led. I always felt sorry for them so I would go talk to them through the fence. We worked out a plan to play through the fence. Some of my friends and I would make a playhouse outside their fence and they would make one on the inside, we would make mud pies. Sometimes we were lucky enough to have real food. My uncle James would always give me money to buy goodies for my friends and me.

He was always proud of me! He thought I was a pretty little girl. I remember how we use to line up so he could see our report cards. I always got on the end so he could really marvel over my good report.

When he got to me he would say, "Let me see how well you've done Lil." I would give him my card feeling proud because I had good grades. He would say, "What's this?" with a frown like something was wrong, and then he would smile showing his beautiful white even teeth. He would then give us money for cold drinks and Joe Louis cookies.

Well, the weather was a lot cooler in the mornings and at night so that meant sweater time. I didn't mind that, because we all had new sweaters to show off. The old ones we had worn the year before last, and last year were outgrown and had to be passed down. We knew to be careful not to ruin them, because money was scarce and everyone had to help each other in our neighborhood. We were one big family; we were united in good times, bad times and in between times. God had been in the mist of us all of the time!

Well, the leaves on the trees are changing; the colors are beautiful. The air is fresh with the smell of autumn. As I look around me, I see neat rows of shotgun houses (that means everything is straight back) whether it's three or four rooms. Then I look at the houses that had more rooms to house larger families all of the yards were neat and clean, because they were swept everyday.

My mother's cousin came up from Georgia to live with us. She had left her mean husband to start her life over. My great-uncle was her father, and she looked just like him. She talked real sweet and was a heavy set woman with extra large breasts and was as neat and clean as she could be, but if you made her mad she could change her voice to a mean gruff tone, which amazed me.

I'd look at her and ask, "Aunt Millie, how do you do that", and she'd look at me and ask "do what?"

I'd stand my ground; look her straight in her eyes and say, "Change like you do."

She'd laugh and say, "Gal, you ask too many questions" and give me a big hug. I'd leave her alone thinking to myself grown folks sure are funny. Oh, well I'm going to be different when I get grown.

We were real busy at school with our lessons and getting ready for our Thanksgiving party. We were drawing, cutting out and coloring, pumpkins, fruit, turkeys and Pilgrims to decorate our windows and around our black board. We were excited because we were going to have sandwiches, cup cakes, milk, candy, and fruit at our homeroom party. Our teacher would let us laugh and talk. It was really a fun time.

We'd go to chapel for our Thanksgiving play. We were proud of our friends that were in the play and we'd cheer them on. I always wanted to be in the play on special occasions, but I was told that I was too black. I could sing pretty and they put me in the glee club, but never to lead a song, which I wanted to do, but I'd say to myself, "I won't be denied." So while I did my chores, I'd sing and go through the parts of the play that I liked, and I felt good about myself.

I was a puzzle to my teachers and even my friends. They would say they never know what I was thinking. I just accepted things, kept on going, walking with my head high or at an angle. That was to let them know that I knew the power of prayer, because I had been taught at an early age that Jesus was in control and would take care of me.

Oh yes, they were right about that, because I knew who was holding my hand and leading me into a future to help people beyond my wildest dreams. Oh no, "I wont' be denied!"

Mommie got an extra job so she could save to get us a house by ourselves. She had a friend she had a lot of confidence in because the lady was good to all of the kids in the neighborhood. She couldn't seem to carry her babies after she got pregnant.

On the nights Mommie had to work late, I had to stay at her house because Aunt Millie worked too. She was very good to me, but one night I woke up to find my gown up to my shoulder and Miss Nice had locked her legs around me, holding me in a position rubbing her wetness on my buttocks moaning, panting and groaning like an animal. It scared me to death almost! The more I tried to get a loose the tighter she held on.

Finally, she finished and I was crying and telling her to get that sticky stuff off of my buttocks. She tried to talk to me and hug me but I wouldn't listen at nothing she said.

After a while she just got quiet, grab me by the hand, took me into the kitchen poured hot water in the wash pan which was steaming hot, cooled it off with cold water out of the water bucket, took down the

"I Won't Be Denied"

octagon soap, and said, "Come on baby, let Miss Nice clean you up."

"Uh, oh". I said I'd do it myself. When I finished, I told her I wanted to go home.

"You have to wait until tomorrow. Now lie down and go to sleep."

When she got in the bed I scooted over to the other side and you can believe my eyes were wide-awake! The next morning she got up and cooked, tried to get me to eat, but I said a firm "no thank you, I just want to go home."

I'm sure I scared her because she said, "I'm going to buy you a pretty outfit this weekend. Now sit down sweetie; I made a mistake. You see grown ups make mistakes like children so please don't tell your mother. I'm so sorry I scared you. I'll make it up to you and don't tell your friends. Don't look at me like that sweetie. I don't want you to hate me."

In my mind I said to myself, "I can't stand you and I'll never trust you again", but with my mouth I said, "Yes, Miss Nice."

Sure enough, that weekend she came over with a beautiful green and white princess style dress, green socks, green ribbon and Sunday school money. I looked at the beautiful clothes and Sunday school money then back at her and I could see the pleading in her eyes so I said, "Thank you, Miss Nice; they're very pretty", and off I went to play.

She seemed very nervous and she had good reason to be because if my Mommie had known what she had done, that would have been the end of her.

Mommie was a good friend to her and very nice to all of the people in our neighborhood. She shared food, clothes, etc., with them to help out. Most of them had more kids and was happy to get what Mommie shared. My mother's brother, Uncle James to me, loves us a lot, he was very proud of us, and we loved him to. He would buy cases of nuts and hard candies and fruit, which Mommie would divide and share with the other families.

Well, the cold weather has set in, it's raining very hard, and that means we kids can't go outside to play. Oh well, "I won't be denied." I'm going to practice my reading and writing because Mommie said this is very important.

"I Won't Be Denied"

As I practiced, I can hear the rain beating on the roof and I began to hum and sing a tune that I just made up to the beat of the raindrops beating on the roof. I thought about the phrase that I heard the ladies in the neighborhood make, so I began to hum and sing "I won't be denied", I won't be denied, because the blacker the berry, the sweeter the juice, because when I get grown I'm going to sing and dance too. I'm going to buy me a chicken and fry it too, and then I'm going to sit down and eat as much as the grown folks do, hum, hum, hum, hum."

You see I really love fried chicken, so that is why I planned to buy, fry and eat as much as I wanted. Mommie always fed me well and she always places two pieces of fried chicken on my plate, but I had to eat my vegetables too. By the time I did that, I was too full to eat anymore. So I planned to just eat chicken.

Since it is Saturday, Mommie and Aunt Millie are out in the kitchen planning Sunday's dinner of chicken dressing, collard greens, potato salad, sweet potato cobbler and corn bread. I was always glad to hear that we were going to have greens so I could break my corn bread into a good hot cup of pot licker. Aunt

Millie always said it was healthy for you and I wanted to stay healthy. I always felt sad when I heard that someone was sick and was eager to go with Mommie and Aunt Millie and the other ladies to help that family out.

Oh well, its Saturday night and the tin tub has been placed near the wood and cold stove in the kitchen so I can take my bath. After my bath, I helped Mommie lay my clothes out for Sunday school and church. Out came my undershirt, snuggies, slip, knee socks, wool skirt, Sunday blouse, sweater, Sunday oxfords, coat, hat, and wool gloves. My bangs rolled with brown paper sack and twisted. I put on my nightclothes, say my prayers, and go off to bed to think how good it'll be to see my friends.

"Goodnight Mommie, Aunt Millie, Uncle James."

Gee, this bed feels good with all of this cover on me. I love a lot of cover because I'm cold natured. I woke up to find Mommie out of bed and the smell of coffee also the squeaking noise of the oven being opened to check on the great biscuits Mommie could make and my special hoe cake of bread she always made me. I knew she truly loved me and was proud of me, but if only she would just hug, kiss, and say the magic words of "I love you baby"! Instead, she took very good care of me, pat me on my cheek, arm, or on the head, and smiled and would say, "Be good, have a good time."

As I walked outside to get with my friends I'd think, when I have children I'm going to tell them how much I love them, hug them, and kiss them so they'll never feel that emptiness I feel. As I grew to be a teenager, I understood Mommie more. She showed her love the only way she knew how. I loved her dearly. She was pretty and I was proud of her, as I stated before.

As me and my friends greeted each other, we were all trying to talk at one time. We had so much to talk about since the last time we saw each other. As we entered the church, we spoke to everyone and took our seats, waiting eagerly for the music to start so we could try to out sing each other, then go to our class where we were given Sunday school cards that had pictures of what the lesson was about. We were also eager to see who would get the attendance banner.

Oh, those were good times! Sunday school is over and church is about to begin. The deacons are getting in place to start praying. The musician is seated at the piano; people are filing in to take their favorite seats.

Everyone is dressed up in their Sunday best smiling and greeting each other. Now the hymn singing has started by the deacon that's going to pray first, after which everyone else joins in; the hymn ends and the praying starts and ends. The musician starts playing and in marches the choir, swaying from side to side. Some of us join in and sing along with them. This is the part I like best because "I won't be denied."

I sing till my heart's content as the choir sings an A & B selection. The preacher gets up makes a few statements and sits down after a lot of amen's. Then it's time for the collection to be taken up and another prayer giving thanks for the collection. The choir sings again and so do I, right along with them. Then the preacher asks everyone to join in with him singing "Amazing Grace." Then he preaches fire and brimstone that touches everyone under the sound of his booming voice. The doors of the church are open and the choir sings, "Come to Jesus." A few people join in and the shouting starts.

I get kind of nervous as the ushers and the ladies sitting near her holding her shoulder, tries to contain her by fanning and holding her while someone says hallelujah let her have her way. The preacher talks a little more telling something funny to make the congregation laugh, then he dismisses church.

Everyone starts talking at once, saying "Chile, we sure had church this morning." Rev. sure preached the truth; it hit us all.

Another lady would answer, "Yes Lord!"

Away we would run playing tag for a while. As we drew near home, we would ask each other what we were having for dinner.

Before we went into the house, we would tell each other what time we would be ready to go back to BYPU that evening.

Our family enjoyed eating dinner together. After dinner, I would jump up and start clearing the table before the phrase of, "Thank the Lord and Bless the cook and I don't care who washes the dishes" was quoted. Now the beginning, "Thank the Lord and Bless the Cook" was fine because I was, and still is thankful for what the Lord has blessed me and my family with. It was the part about "I don't care who wash the dishes" that I didn't like, because I was the one who had to do the dishes, except rare occasions.

Today was one of them. Mommie smiled that beautiful smile and told me I could go visit my friends across the street for a while. She and Aunt Millie began to clean the kitchen up, talking and laughing like two schoolgirls.

It's another school day, the same routine; the same long walk to school. Oh well, we'll soon be out for Christmas and we're all talking about what we wanted Santa Claus to bring us.

Even though we knew that it was our parents that brought us the goodies, we just pretend that Santa was the real deal. That way we got more. After we let our parents know we knew better, all of the excitement was gone concerning Santa.

Gee, the house smelled wonderful with the baking of cakes and pies. I use to wait to get the spoon and bowl after Mommie and Aunt Millie emptied it into the cake, and pie pans. They always cooked me

"I Won't Be Denied"

a sample so I wouldn't have to wait until Christmas to enjoy the wonderful desserts.

It's the morning of Christmas Eve and you can believe all of the houses in our neighborhood are all a flutter.

At our house, Uncle James was teasing me saying, "Lil, have you been a real good girl so Santa Claus can drop by here tonight?" I looked at him and smiled and said, "Uncle James, you know I have. I've done my chores, made good grades, gone to Sunday school, church, and BYPU and I say my prayers all of the time. Do you think I'll get something extra for all of these nice things I've done and you know I always mind?"

He looked at me smiling and said, Yeah Lil, you are a good little girl maybe there will be something extra for you."

Uncle James and I walked to the kitchen to see what else Mommie and Aunt Millie was fixing good to eat. I said to my self that I wish the extra could be a beautiful blue bicycle. Blue was my favorite color, but truthfully, I knew that would never happen because every since Little Brother was killed, Mommie was afraid of something would happen to me. Sometime when Mommie was sitting quietly in a deep study, I'd wish I could make her completely happy, but being young, I didn't realize that it was out of my hands.

Oh boy, it's time to eat! We're having collard greens, spaghetti and meatballs, corn bread, and candied yams. Aunt Millie said, "You're a big girl; get you a cup and get your own pot licker. I declare she loves that stuff better than a hog loves slop." I stopped dipping my pot licker and looked at her real hard and she said, "No gal, I'm not calling you a hog. I was just saying you really love that stuff called pot licker." Everyone laughed; even I gave a weak laugh. I thought, sometimes I wonder about grownups. Oh well, I know they love me and I don't care what they say--except about the dishes.

After the kitchen was cleaned up and the food put away I went in and began to get ready for bed and to listen to the radio for a while. Seems like it took me forever to go to sleep. I woke up early Christmas morning and heard the grown ups out in the kitchen laughing and talking.

"I Won't Be Denied"

I jumped out of bed and stuck my head into the kitchen to find them drinking coffee. Gee, it really smelled good, but grown ups always said coffee made you black, but I know that was to keep it for themselves.

Well I'm all dressed and ready to open my gifts and eat my good breakfast of hoecake bread, cheese, and hot sassafras tea. Oh my, look at the beautiful skirts and sweaters four of each, two slips and panties, socks, new saddle oxfords, gloves, new hat and coat for Sunday! Now I could wear my old Sunday coat and hat to school and pass my school coat and hat on to someone else because I am really growing.

I went to Mommie and gave her a big hug and said, "Thank you a whole lot for my beautiful clothes Mommie; I love you."

She smiled and said, "You're welcome. Now take care of them."

Then Aunt Millie said, "Here's something else for you, I hope you like them."

Eagerly, I tore the paper off to find two under shirts and a pretty white blouse with little rosettes on the collar and down the front that had been embroidered on.

I gave her a big hug and told her, "Thank you Aunt Millie and I love you too"!

She got a little teary and said, "I love you too gal and you're shore welcome."

Uncle James was still asleep and I wanted him to wake up so I cold see what he had for me. I kept walking in and out of the front room where he slept, but he continued to sleep. I wondered if he was hungry.

Finally, I couldn't stand it anymore so I just tickled his foot and said, "Merry Christmas Uncle James."

He yawned with one eye opened saying, "Good morning Lil. Was Santa Claus good to you?"

I said, "Oh yes, get up so you can come and see what I have."

He told me to go and tell sis (that's what he called Mommie) to fix him two eggs. "I'll be right there."

I told Mommie and she fixed his eggs and bacon (streak-a-lean) of course, biscuits, and coffee. I

"I Won't Be Denied"

kept watching him and he just kept eating and smiling. I sat down at the table across from him trying to be patient, but I just couldn't any longer.

I looked straight at him and said, "Uncle James, you know today is Christmas, did you forget the extra you were talking about?"

He answered me by asking, "Is it really Christmas Lil?" By then, I was fit to be tied! He had never forgotten me before.

I got up and said, "I've got to go to help make up the beds and empty the slop jars."

As I walked to the door he said, "Lil here's the extra", and handed me a present wrapped real nice. I thought it sure is little, but I said, "Thank you, Uncle James."

He said, "Aren't you going to open it?"

"Oh, yes sir"! I opened it to find a pretty Mickey Mouse watch. I just stood there and said, "Thank you, thank you, thank you Uncle James for my extra gift; it's really nice"!

"You're more than welcome Lil", he said with that smile that showed his beautiful teeth. I went to show off my beautiful extra gift to Mommie and Aunt Millie. They smiled and said it was very nice.

Now that I had collected all of my gifts, I went and got the three gifts out of my box where I kept my treasures to give Mommie, Aunt Millie and Uncle James. I watched each one as they opened their gifts.

Mommie's eyes filled with water and she looked at me like I was heaven sent and said, "Thank you. It's very pretty." It was a pretty white handkerchief with rosettes in one corner.

Aunt Millie's was a box of snuff (because she dipped). She said, "Thank you gal; you're a sweet chile."

Uncle James said, "Why Lil, you mean you had Santa Claus to bring us a nice gift", and he unwrapped a pair of white socks because his feet were bad and he had to always wear white socks. I felt real proud of myself!

Well it's time to visit my friends to see what Santa had left them.

"Mommie, may I go over to my friend's houses to see what they've got and bring them back to see mine?"

"Yes, you may."

"Bye"--out the door I went like a shot! Gee, it's sure cold out here. I began to run so I could stay warm. I knocked on the door of Annie's house; she answered with a big grin.

"Hi Lillian, come see, come see what we got for Christmas. Girl, we're going to get ready for Sunday school real early Sunday, what did you get?"

All of this was said almost in the same voice. "Oh, Annie", I said, "They are pretty." There were skirts, sweaters, socks, shoes, panties etc. I was glad she and her brother and sister were happy!

Well Thanksgiving and Christmas is over and all is well. It's New Year's Eve and I'm helping Mommie and Aunt Millie in the kitchen. I'm picking black-eyed peas; Mommie is cutting streak-a-lean to cook the peas and the collard greens. Aunt Millie was cleaning and cutting them up.

I felt real special as we laughed, talked and sipped sassafras tea while we worked. We were having cole slaw, chitterlings, and candied yams to go with the peas and collards.

I loved to cook and set the table with our special dishes that were used on special occasions. We're having homemade vegetable soup for supper with good hot corn bread. All leftovers that we'd had during the week were used to make a fine pot of soup. The other food was ready for New Years dinner tomorrow.

Gee, I'm full and I'm ready to listen to the radio before getting ready for bed. I finished washing the soup bowls quickly so I could go listen to the radio. It's really cold weather now and we could hear the wind blowing, but it's nice and warm inside. The next morning I was awakened by loud knocks on the door.

I heard Aunt Millie say, "Who is it?"

"It's me, Thomas. I came to walk through you all's house for good luck."

Aunt Millie was overjoyed because she was sweet on him and he liked her a lot. After he walked through, he looked and saw I was awake said, "Morning Lil; you getting your beauty rest?"

I said, "Good morning. Yes sir, I am" and he went to the kitchen for an enjoyable breakfast.

"I Won't Be Denied"

Oh, boy, we're having liver, onions, gravy, rice, and biscuits! I got in a rush, washed my face, brushed my teeth, and jumped in my clothes so I could eat and watch Aunt Millie blush every time she and Mr. Thomas looked at each other. It always tickled me the way she would eat a little amount while he was there, but as soon as he left, her appetite zoomed. Mommie would look at me, smile, and shake her head for me not to say anything about it. I'd just sit and watch her. I guess she knew I wanted to ask her why she didn't eat enough when Mr. Thomas was there, because she'd look at me out the corner of her eyes and say, "What are you looking at gal?"

I'd look at Mommie before I'd answer, "I'm just looking at you eat all of that food."

She and Mommie would laugh and laugh until their stomachs hurt. Then Mommie would say, "Go make up the bed Lillian."

"Yes ma'am." Then I'd think to myself again that grow-ups sure are funny.

Well it's spitting snow and the weather is cold. I'm really growing and beginning to enjoy reading and learning everything, and I care about being more lady-like. I love going to the picture show (movies), watching the beautiful ladies in their pretty furs and clothes; also the pearls were nice. I'd stay and see the movies twice just to pretend that I was wearing all of those pretty things. After I got out of the movies I'd think to myself and again vow, "I won't be denied", because I'm going to have all of those wonderful things when I get grown.

It seems like time flies! I'm in junior high school and being extra careful how I dress and wear my hair. I always try to be on my best behavior. I can dance and sing real well and my grades are good. I have lots of friends plus I've got a job promised to me at the swimming pool at Lincoln Park when school is out for the summer. I'm going to save all of my money except for three dollars to buy my special goodies with.

Well it's time for our tests and everyone is a flutter trying to study for exams. Our teacher has entered the room and is looking around the room smiling.

"Good morning children."

"Good morning, teacher."

She looked so pretty with her navy blue dress with the pretty white-collar and black pumps. Her hair is in a neat, clinging ball and bangs, and she has on pearl ear screws (earrings). She began writing on the black board. When she finished, she said, "Now children, you may begin; no talking or cheating."

I said a little prayer asking God to help me. I began to work on my test and praise God! It seemed so easy. I finished ahead of time and looked over it to make sure I had done everything that needed doing.

"Lillian, you and Evelyn take up the test papers so we can get our next assignments out." Oh boy, its lunchtime and I'm really ready to eat! Evelyn and I headed for the cafeteria so we could get in line before it gets too long. We could smell the wonderful soup and could hardly wait to get ours. We would buy our own lunches, but we would get one carton of milk and share it. We were very close and had a lot of fun.

When our school burned, we had to go to Howard High a little earlier in the morning. We missed our old school a lot! Mrs. Hayden had a paddle she named Ben and she really used it if you cut up. We could hardly wait to hear Mrs. Hayden say it time for our current events then she would call on us to recite.

One morning she called on George. He had stolen some of his daddy's whiskey and drank it; he was high as a kite! He was also red as a beet!

When Mrs. Hayden called on him he had not studied and didn't have a current event to give so he just stood up and said, "For my current event today, I read where Jesse James was shot", and sat down.

The whole class took one look at Mrs. Hayden, then back at George and laughed until Mrs. Hayden had to laugh too. He thought he had done something cute. It was so funny the way he did it. We all loved Mrs. Hayden a lot! She loved us too!

Well it's prom time and we're a flutter waiting on someone to ask to take us to the prom. Finally, we were all asked. Mommie bought me a beautiful blue evening gown at Lynch's Boutique. I had me a pair of shoes tinted the same color, a beautiful bow and I had a cute beaded bag with a rhinestone clasp.

I was so happy--then doom struck. The boy that had asked me decided that he wanted to take one of our classmates who was real light. He said I was real cute

"I Won't Be Denied"

and dressed nice, but I was too black and back then, being called "black" was fighting words.

After hearing about this, I told him I had heard he wanted to carry someone else, "So you do just that; I don't want to go with you!"

He looked real funny and asked, "Who told you?"

I said, "None of your business", and walked away.

Now I had to tell Mommie, which I hated to do because she had worked hard to dress me up for the prom, but I told her. Of course I was ashamed to face my friends without an escort, but Mommie said, "Lillian, life is hard, sometimes people can say or do things that'll hurt you real bad, but always remember you are just as good as anyone else. Hold your head up; go on to the prom tomorrow night."

Uncle James drove me to the prom and gave me a beautiful corsage. He said, "Lil, you look beautiful!"

"Thank you, Uncle James."

Mommie was real proud of me and was smiling that wonderful smile of hers. I felt great! When I got out of the car, I waved goodbye to Uncle James and said thank you again. When I walked in, the music sounded good and everyone looked nice. My friends came toward me grinning and were glad to see me.

They said, "Girl you sure look pretty."

"Thanks."

Some of the guys who also came stag kept me real busy dancing. I really had a good time! I spoke to my previous escort who had conked out on me and his date really nice. He couldn't look at me straight.

He said, "You sure look nice Lillian," and I said, "Thank you. You do too" and I meant it.
Again, "I won't be denied."

The last song was played and it was time to go. I said my goodbyes and went outside to see Uncle James waiting for me.

"Did you enjoy yourself Lil?"

"Oh, yes sir!" I answered. "I had a real good time."

I was full of good news when I got home. Mommie and Aunt Millie were all ears. After I finished my news of the prom, I pulled off my beautiful clothes and put them up. I got into my nightclothes, said my

"I Won't Be Denied"

prayers, and went to bed but not to sleep for a long time. I was still excited over my evening of beautiful clothes, dancing and chatting with my friends. Finally, I fell off to sleep. Gee, I was more tired than I thought I was. I slept until nine o'clock.

Um, something sure smells good coming from the kitchen. Fried potatoes, onions, sausages, biscuits, homemade jelly, and, of course, coffee for the grown ups.

Gee, I'm really growing up and life is still good for me and Mommie. Aunt Millie is still sweet on Mr. Thomas and of course, he liked her even more than she knew because he didn't do much love talk to her, but he would have a funny look on his face if he saw other men talking to her.

He would ease up and say, "How y'all doing?" with a half smile and say, "Miss Millie, you reckon I could get you to fix me a bite of supper tonight? I'll pay whatever you charge", knowing good and well there were no charges.

She'd answer with a big smile and say, "We'll see; come on over Thomas," and boy, she would fry corn, steam cabbage, par boil and crisp fat back bacon, sliced tomatoes, onion and corn cakes (fried corn bread), and make iced tea. He'd eat and look at Aunt Millie like she was the queen of Sheba. I saw a lot of love for years between them looking at each other or holding hands. They were like two teenagers. That's what the world needed then and what the world needs now is a lot of wholesome love.

As I look around, I see the trees budding and Mother Nature doing an artful job by the mighty grace of God! Now that spring has sprung, all of the children in the neighborhood are happy to be outside laughing, talking and playing after being cooped up in the house during the winter months. I noticed my friends are really growing up, and our parents are still working hard trying to make ends meet. The trees are budding, flowers blooming, sap rising and the birds are singing gleefully. It feels wonderful to walk outside, stretch and look around at the neat row of houses with their dirt yard being swept, porches scrubbed, the ladies that are fortunate enough to be able to stay at home, but help out by taking in washing and ironing.

The children are nice and clean, hair combed; the ladies dressed in starched ironed print dresses, hair neat, pretty aprons. The men gone to work dressed mostly in their starched ironed overalls that have been neatly patched where they have worn out, to make them last longer.

Easter is almost here, and we're excited about the Easter Egg Hunt and, of course, our new clothes. Friday night Mommie washed my hair and put a little hair grease on it, brushed it until it was nice and easy to manage then she platted it in four plaits.

The next morning was Saturday and I got up early so I wouldn't be late getting to the beauty parlor (shop). Everybody was in high spirits laughing, talking, and exchanging small talk about their new clothes and where they were going. I always enjoyed going to the beauty shop to watch the hairdressers as they were called in those days, but they're called beauticians now. They knew the right amount of heat and pressure to put on different textures of hair to get beautiful results. After I became a teenager, I started wearing my hair in a pageboy and I was really excited about it because I could keep my own hair rolled, combed and brushed myself.

As time moved on things began to change, more and more people that we were use to seeing and talking to died and some families moved to another part of the city and some out of town. These were sad times for everyone. In my heart, I knew that I would always hold the precious memories in my heart. They were really missed and for those that still lived in the city, we could hardly wait until we could see each other whenever we could visit. Oh yes, there were good times, bad times and in between times that kept us so close.

Well it's Saturday and there's no school today, but it'll be a busy day because I'll get all of my school clothes ready for the upcoming week polish my saddle oxfords and shine my black shoes just in case it rains. I love matching my skirts, sweater, socks and ribbons up. Aunt Millie is going to wash my hair after I finish my clothes, then off to my favorite place (the beauty shop).

It never ceases to amaze me how the ladies would come to get their hair fixed and try to out brag each other. It was their way of forgetting their troubles. It made them feel beautiful getting their hair fixed, and beautiful they were in their own way. As I looked at them I thought wouldn't it be wonderful if they could be this happy all of the time. Life for most people is hard and it's a blessing to be able to soften it, if only a little bit.

Well it's my time to get in the chair.

"Hi Lillian."

"Hi, Miss Rivers."

"How's school?"

"Fine", I'd always say. Then she asked me how I wanted my hair fixed that day.

"Bangs, and turned under."

Then the conversation would start again with the ladies. As one of the ladies got out of one of the other hairdresser's chair all of the other ladies would marvel over the way she looked.

She'd take the mirror and look at the back of her head and smile broadly and said, "Chile, my man sho gonna like this hair do!" then she'd do a little dance and shake her hips and say, "Ta ta girls, see you in church" and off she'd go. Then the talk would really start.

Girl, she is sho nuff in love with that husband of hers and he's in love with every skirt he sees, but she looks better than any of those bats I've seen him with.

Another lady would chime in and say, "Chile it don't matter none because he do take of home, and she's not worrying that much because she knows if he runs long enough he'll come home wagging his tail behind him."

Then they'd laugh until tears came into their eyes, and down their cheeks, then they'd all would say, "Yeah, that's for sho."

As another lady would leave, they'd start on her and so on. Sometimes I'd wonder, as I'd walk home from the beauty shop if they'd do me that way. I felt they had something to say and sure enough, Sunday evening when we got out of church and have our dinner and we would be sitting on the front porch one of the ladies would come over, sit, and talk with Mommie and Aunt Millie.

As she walked up, she'd say evening girls, "How's tricks?"

They'd say "pretty good" as they smiled broadly and tell her to come on up and sit a spell.

"I Won't Be Denied"

She'd smile and say, "Don't mind if I do."

"Hey Lillian."

I'd answer and say, "Hey Miss Rose."

Mommie would say, "Lillian, go get Miss Rose a glass of lemonade" and of I'd go, return with the lemonade "Here, Miss Rose."

"Thank you, dear chile. They tell me everybody is crazy about Lillian down at the beauty shop. Say she a mannerable chile. I know y'all proud of her."

Mommie and Aunt Millie would smile and say, "Thank you, Rose."

"Go play, Lillian." As I'd leave, I heard Mommie say, "She does real good, but I don't want her to get the big head that's why I told her to go play."

Aunt Millie would say, "Yeah, you have to be careful with chaps."

I would walk slow and stop looking up and down the street like I was looking for my playmates.

Miss Rose would say, "They went down by your cousin's house."

Off I would go with Mommie saying loudly, "Be back in time to go to BYPU Lillian." "Yes ma'am."

Now that most of my friends and their families had moved away I felt lonely and wondered if they felt the same way too. Life didn't seem as adventurous as it did before. Sometimes I would just walk around the neighborhood and look at the pretty flowers and gardens that the neighbors had planted and was always amazed at the way the Lord would let things grow to feed families and to enjoy the beauty of the flowers that grew.

How it that there are so many people and God is is in control of everything? I'm so glad that me and Mommie know the truth; that God is real and "I won't be denied" my blessings because I trust him for everything.

One day Mommie came home from work all smiles and said that they had finished the housing projects on the west side and she was going to apply for one for me and her. Aunt Millie didn't want to move from the neighborhood so she got her a rented house next to the store on Chestnut Street, made it into a boarding house, starting renting rooms. She was really happy because she felt useful. We all hated to part, but were happy for each other and about our new lives.

Of course, we visited each other often and as usual, it was a joyous time when we got together. Mommie would cook Aunt Millie's favorite food when she'd come visiting us: Croaker fish (fried), mashed potatoes, cole slaw, corn bread, and lemonade.

I always enjoyed the meal too, but, oh boy, I would jump for joy when it was our time to go out to Aunt Millie's because she would have told everyone we knew that were still in the old neighborhood that we were coming! She'd make sure she had plenty of fried chicken, hot biscuits, gravy, rice home made jelly and lemonade because she knew I love fried chicken and rice and my special hoe cake (biscuit) bread she and Mommie always made me.

She'd look at me and say, "Ain't she the cutest thing and my how she's growing", and Mommie, of course, would say, "Yes, she really is growing up with a lot of pride", and gee I would feel so special because I really loved Mommie and Aunt Millie too.

We would really hate leaving, but Uncle James would carry us home before he went to work. He was still in the old house, but he was proud of Mommie moving into a nicer place. It was very nice and our new neighbors were nice too, plus they had children around my age that made things greater.

All of the young people were in high spirits because of the upcoming block party on 14th Street. It was an annual thing that everyone enjoyed, even the older folks. The Street would be blocked off near a little café where you could buy sandwiches, cold drinks and the music would be played, and everyone would really eat, dance, talk, and enjoy themselves. We could hardly wait to get there. It was only about three blocks from where we lived, yet it seemed like I couldn't get there fast enough. Sometimes I would run all the way there. I loved to dance and sing as I said before. The music was magical to me and you can believe I would dance and sing until my heart was content! After it was over, we would stand around and talk awhile then head for home, thinking about the fun time we'd had.

There was a boy in our new neighborhood that I really liked. He was neat and well dressed and all of the girls liked him. He would cut up with them, having fun, but there was always a serious look on his face when he'd speak to me.

"I Won't Be Denied"

Sometimes when Mommie would send me to the corner store or if I wanted something, I'd see him. Most of the time, he would be standing across the street at his friend's house looking at me with that serious expression.

One day he got enough nerve to say, "Hey, (with a slow drawl), do you receive company yet?" And I said, 'No, not yet."

He smiled and said, 'Ok, I'll see you later."

My heart did flip-flops! I said to myself, "Gee, he sure is cute." Well I was crushed when I saw him with another girl. Everyone said they're really going together and that was that. After that, Mommie would let me have company.

The years seemed to fly and I started going to the football games. I met my first husband. He was truly a star. He was tall dark and very handsome, nice grade of hair, big eyes with the longest eyelashes that curled up. He was 6 ft 1 in, very smart in school and we got along great. We'd dance and talk about everything. Mommie really liked him because he was very mannerable. Everything was going great and I was making plans to go to college.

Then Uncle James was shot to death. Mommie was ironing upstairs in our bedroom and I was folding and putting the towels and under clothes away when we received the terrible news. I'll never forget the look on Mommie's face. We both were crushed. After that, Mommie was never the same.

His brother-in-law had shot him in the back. He was at the filling station getting gas when it happened. A man that worked there said Uncle James had a surprised look of shock on his face and asked his brother-in-law, "Why are you doing this?" and fell.

The brother-in-law said, "I was told you were gonna get me", which wasn't true. It was something happened between him and my aunt (my uncle's wife), but she never told my uncle.

The funeral was very sad, our relatives and friends were screaming and wailing. I was crying and shaking all over. It seem like I could hear him say, "Don't cry, Lil. Don't be afraid; everything will be all right."

I made up my mind I would be brave for him. But Mommie got worse. She began to talk to herself and do strange things. Like one day, I came home from school and she had not gone to work and had peeled potatoes and thrown the peelings on the eyes of the stove.

She would also hold both of my hands so tight until they would swell, because she thought someone was going to hurt me. I'd just sit there all day until she decided to release me. It broke my heart to see her like this.

I had to call my aunt (her sister) to come and help me. Aunt Millie was sick; she never got over my uncle's death either. When my aunt got here, she had to put Mommie in the hospital.

When they carried her in, her nerves were so bad until her hair stood out from her head like electricity was in it. It frightened me so bad I just cried and prayed that God would answer my prayers and make her better. Then a decision had to be made about me, and I wanted to stay near Mommie. So I got married.

I will never forget the kindness that was shown to me by Aunt Ceil and Aunt Myrtle. They made me feel good about myself. I'll always cherish the fond memories of the love that was showered upon me. The wonderful feeling of waiting for the good homemade chili that simmered on the heater that threw out the warmth that enveloped us as we waited for Aunt Ceil and Aunt Myrtle to say, "It's ready to eat", and me and my best friend, Cousin Ginny would look at each other, smile, get our bowls, spoons and crackers and eat until our hearts were content. Aunt Ceil would braid our hair in different pretty styles and just dress us up. They were wonderful women, full of love. I wish everyone could have had someone in their lives like them.

Sometimes I look around me and say to myself, "Gee, how things have changed from manual to automatic, from walking to riding etc. Yet, we seem to go in the wrong direction instead of the right one. Certainly, God has blessed us in a mighty way. Instead of being thankful, we seem to feel like the world owes us everything on a silver platter.

I was 18 when I got married, in love, and excited about playing housewife--washing, ironing, cooking and all of the duties of a wife, but I soon found out that it was no play; it was the real deal.

My husband worked for a good company and made a fairly decent salary. We were both young and didn't really know too much about budgeting so things began to go down hill. You can't live on love alone.

We were thrilled when we found out I was pregnant! We began to watch our money closer. Finally, the blessed day of the birth of our beautiful baby girl came, 8lbs 3oz. and she was worth all of the pain I suffered. Certainly, she was an adorable, curly headed doll. Thank God for our healthy baby girl.

Things got rough again-- bills, food, diapers, formulas, etc. My husband came home and asked me to go with him. He seemed upset, but he kept saying there was nothing wrong. In my heart, I knew something wasn't right, but I kept quiet and off we went downtown.

I'll never forget the awful feeling in the pit of my stomach, as he said "I'll be right back, wait for me here," and off he went into the building at 9:00 o'clock in the morning. I waited patiently outside of the building until 3:00 o'clock in the afternoon. I was so tired and hungry plus worried about my baby. I had left her with my mother-in-law. By now I knew she was fuming thinking we were goofing off.

As he walked toward me he looked at me and said, "Pumpkin, I've just joined the Air Force. I made an allotment out for you and Kay."

I almost fainted, I wanted to scream, cry and run until I could clear my head from this awful thing that was happening to me. Instead of giving in to this feeling, I made up my mind "I won't be denied", so, as usual, I asked God to give me strength to endure whatever was to come. As I walked home alone, silent tears rolled down my cheeks. I stopped by my mother-in-law's house to tell her what had happened and to give her the message her son, my husband had sent.

"Tell mother not to worry; I'm fine. I'll write you soon Pumpkin; kiss Kay for me." After I told her what had happened, she said it might be the best thing for him.

She didn't have any idea how alone, miserable and scared I was with no money, bills due food low and no one to turn to for help. I had taken cosmetology in high school so I began to do all my neighbors hair, charging $3.00 a head, which went a long way toward our upkeep.

"I Won't Be Denied"

I was shocked to find out that I didn't get a check like my husband had said; only to find out he hadn't included us after all. But to make things worse in, I was pregnant again; that meant three mouths to feed. My mother-in-law told me to go to the Red Cross and have them get in touch with my husband, so I could get a check. I was blessed with a nice lady waiting on me and she went right to work on my case. Thank God! The next month, my check arrived. I was able to pay my bills, buy food, etc. and have extra money for emergencies with the money I made doing hair, plus my check. What a relief it was to relax my mind instead of worrying.

We lived around the corner from my mother-in-law and she use to cook lunch for the people that worked at the factory, school and other places near by. She was a great cook and I loved helping her. I met a lot of nice people that came for lunch. Her best friend worked at the factory and she would bring someone with her to help carry the ordered lunches back. We would pack their lunches in a box that would hold eight lunches and each one would carry a box which meant sixteen plate lunches five days a week at $2.00

a plate. Some of her meals were spaghetti and neck bones, pinto beans, coke slaw, corn bread, apple cobbler, fried chicken, green beans, potato salad, sweet potato cobbler, steamed cabbage, fried corn, meat loaf, and peach cobbler. Some of the people would spend their lunch break there eating and talking. It was very interesting listening at some of the things they would talk about. Some were logical, others were not, but we all have our dreams.

I haven't heard from my husband yet. I think he's a little peeved because I had the Red Cross lady get in touch with his commanding officer. I'm sorry he feels that way, but I have to think about my baby girl (now a toddler) and the one on the way. Oh Lord, I think I've made a drastic mistake! I use to hear Mommie and Aunt Millie say love over looks a million faults and I know what they mean now.

"Oh dear heavenly father, help me to stay strong and be able to raise my children right"! It seems that I'm forever praying and asking God to help me. He's my only hope.

Oh my, how the time does fly, things change, grown ups get older and the kids become teenagers, but it seems that Mommie gets prettier. I love the way she looks when she dresses up. She walks so proud! I often wonder why life couldn't have been better for women like Mommie, Aunt Millie and some of the other women in our old neighborhood and the new ones, just all over the world really. They are all beautiful in their own way. Hard working, proud, sharing, caring, neat and yet they're humble. It seems that the men in their lives rather have the ones that were the hard drinkers, partying kind. Oh well. that's what makes the world go around, the difference in people, and what a difference a day can make.

It was springtime again. I should have been completely happy, but a dark shadow loomed over our house. Mommie began to act a little strange again. One day I came home Mommie was upstairs talking to herself. When I got upstairs, she was just sitting in our bedroom just staring with a bewildered look in her eyes.

I ran to her and said, "What's wrong Mommie, can I help?"

She just stared. I sat on the bed and kept talking to her until she seemed all right but later that week she was talking to herself again, this time smiling in a strange way.

I went to her and said, "Mommie, let's go out to Uncle Lee's and Aunt Ula's house for awhile." I thought if I got her out there, they would help me with her. I was so scared for her. I loved her so much I just wanted things to be ok for her.

Well, help I did get and Aunt Ula put her to bed. She began to talk all through the night. I prayed and worried all night. The next morning Uncle Lee went to work. I heard Aunt Ula talking to her next-door neighbor saying Mommie was crazy. I was devastated beyond words. I thought how could she do this to Mommie who had washed, ironed, cooked, cleaned her house and consoled her when things were dark for her and this is the way she's repaying Mommie.

Later on, she came into the bedroom and said, "You'll have to take her out of here. What will my neighbors say?" I couldn't believe this woman I loved was being this cruel!

I helped Mommie get a bath, combed her beautiful hair and helped her dress. I took her by the hand and led her out into the street to catch a jitney

"I Won't Be Denied"

(cab) to go to town and then to catch a bus to carry Mommie home.

Just before we got to the corner Mommie broke away from me and I caught her, telling her we were going home. A lady was coming up the street saw me having a hard time with her ask me what was wrong. By then, I was almost in tears.

I said, "Lady please help me get my Mommie in the next jitney that comes by", and she said yes. She told me to try and get her to a doctor. We got her in the jitney without any trouble. As we drove away, I looked up the street and saw Aunt Ula and her neighbor looking at us. I vowed that I would never mistreat anyone like this. When we got home, I was so grateful! I prayed and prayed! It's a terrible thing to need someone to stand by you, and they turn away from you without a care.

I asked our neighbor to let me call my Mommie's sister in Philadelphia, Pennsylvania and she said yes. I almost screamed when I heard my aunt's voice. I was crying so hard until Miss Lucille had to take the telephone and talk to her. She said she would leave that night and take a cab to our house. Thank you

Jesus for kind hearted Miss Lucille! Sure enough, Aunt Evelyn (Mommie's sister) arrived and I ran to greet her. Mommie smiled when she saw her and tears came in their eyes as they embraced.

Again, Mommie became disoriented and we had to call an ambulance and take her to the hospital and, again I saw her hair stand out like electricity was in it.

"Oh Jesus, help my Mommie", and he did. The nurse gave her a shot and she quieted down. She looked at me frighten and I went to her and said, "I love you, Mommie; you'll be ok."

Mommie had been through pure hell all of her life. At the age of 14, her mother died, she was sent to live with an aunt, and started working as a domestic to help pay her way. Times were very hard. She got married, had me, my little brother, lost a set of twins, lost another baby, my little brother (Roy) was killed, her marriage had failed before Roy was killed by a car. She fell in love with another cheating man and quit him.

After a long time of being alone, she met Mr. Riley, he died of heart attack, and her brother was shot and killed and now this nervous breakdown. It's a wonder if she lasted this long, but God is good yesterday, today, and forever He came when we needed Him the most. My advice to every one is to trust HIM for his word for He said He'd never leave us and He's never made a promise He didn't keep.

Aunt Evelyn signed Mommie into a place where she could get help. It was pure hell to have to leave her there. I didn't want her to feel like nobody cared about her. After they quieted her down and treated her, they let me visit her. I'd take fruit, candy, books, and money for her to buy cokes until my next visit. She would never talk to me, and I thought it was because she was depressed; but after she got well (which took years) I found out she had lost her voice and didn't want to worry me.

I'll always remember how happy she was when I went to get her. She was full of smiles, and in a hurry to get home. By then, I had five children, Karen (K-K), Janise (Jan), Patricia (Patti), William (Billy), and Raymond Jr (Little Raymond). Let's go back a little.

While Mommie was in the hospital, I got married, with Aunt Evelyn's consent, and had four kids and then my marriage failed. My husband was a fun loving person, young, handsome, very intelligent. As with most young couples, after the bills and babies started coming, things just fell apart. I was lonely, depressed with four kids at this time, but I kept the hope of a better day for my kids, and me but things got worse before they got better.

I didn't have any help with my kids. I worked very hard to keep them up. I got so low until I felt like killing myself. I thought maybe if I were gone my kids could get a check every month, be taken care of, and get the insurance money, but I found out that they wouldn't get any insurance money if I killed myself.

I told a lady that I could confide in how I felt, and she said, "It's always dark before daylight. Trust God."

Right then I looked at her and said "Thank you for listening" and "I won't be denied." I'm going to trust Him, and work harder. I did domestic work during the day, fixed hair at home at night, and sure enough things began to brighten up.

My husband and I were separated and he was out of service, so the checks stopped. I got a job at

"I Won't Be Denied"

the Patten Hotel working as a lobby maid. My friend Marian worked on the mezzanine. We worked the dances and parties as hat and coat checkers. The extra money made life a lot brighter and I was thankful to God for His blessing.

One of the young ladies I use to fix hair told me about a club dance that she had been invited to and asked me to go with her.

I said, "No thank you, maybe next time."

She said, "Girl you never go anyplace, you need to get out of the house sometime."

I thought about what she said after she left, and promised myself the next time I was asked, I would go, and sure enough the next time I was asked, I did go and saw a lot of people I hadn't seen in years. I really enjoyed myself talking and dancing. It really felt good to be footloose and fancy free for a few hours.

I met a nice mannerable young man that kept coming back asking me to dance. He had a nice smile and was really a joy to talk to. He asked to see me again, I told him I didn't get out often, because I had four kids, and I was out because they were visiting their grandparents. Well that didn't bother him at all;

if anything it seemed to encourage him. He asked if he could take me home and I told him that I had come with my friends and I had to stick with them. He just smiled and said, "That's ok. I'll take them too." So, I said yes and true to his word, he took them home first then he took me home.

We sat in his car and talked a long time. He was waiting for his divorce to be final; he had two kids around the same age as mine. I told him it was getting late and I'd better go inside. It was too late for him to come in.

"I'm kind of old fashioned, but you're welcome to come by to meet my kids when they come home Sunday evening."

Sure enough, he came by late Sunday evening the kids had been home awhile and were out playing with their friends. I asked him in and offered him a coke.

He said, "No thanks, I'm ok."

So, we just looked at each other, and smiled, and then he said, "Do you want to go for a ride?"

"Yes, if I can carry my kids too."

"I Won't Be Denied"

He said, "You know you can'. So, I called them home and introduced them to him. They were overjoyed.

We stopped for ice cream cones then rode to look at the beautiful homes. It was a fun evening for us all. He was very nice to me and my kids. His mother would come out and spend time with the kids and me. Everything went well until he spoke about marrying then everything started going bad. His mother started acting funny, didn't come around me, and the kids anymore. Then he started courting on me, and then out of the blue he came by and said he wouldn't be back. I felt like someone had kicked me in the stomach.

That same weekend he drove by my house with his new girlfriend sitting close to him with her arm around his shoulder, as he drove by he saw me sitting on my front porch reading he blew his horn at me. I was really hurt, but I said to myself like I had done many times before "I won't be denied" so I smiled and waved.

My neighbors walked over and said, "Lillian I can't believe he did that to you. You've been so nice to him.

"He'll be sorry one of these days", and sure enough, he was. But I continued to pray and God opened doors for me and I starting dating again.

This time it was with a young man that use to stand and watch me. He came up to me and said, "Hey", in his long drawl way. "I know you're receiving company now" and we both had a big laugh. He was a caring, sharing person, very handsome, neat, and polite. Everything went well until in stepped the devil, which come in all shapes. This time he came in a dress all full of lies because she wanted to be his lady.

Oh well, life is full of disappointments and when they come, we have to be strong and most of all *trust God* and keep on trying to find happiness along the way. I think I'll just stop trying to make life be the way I want it, but just take life as it comes if it's decent and in order, and *thank God* for the special blessing.

Well it's almost 4th of July and all of the kids in the neighborhood are talking about what they want to wear for that day. I had already put my kids' clothes away on the top shelf of the living room closet, back in the corner so they wouldn't see them. I bought my girl's cute shorts, tops, and sandals and my son shorts and shirt with short sleeves and a pair of roman sandals.

When they got up on the 4th of July, I gave them their baths, breakfast, combed their hair, brushed my little boy's hair, and let them go outside to find their friends.

When they came in to get their lunch and take a nap, I had their new outfits laid out. Oh, my you would have thought I had given them all of the candy from the store. They were truly happy. It made me feel good to see them happy. I loved them with every fiber of my being and still do, but I've always loved Jesus first, because he brought me through the seen, and unseen. *Thank you Jesus!*

Then one day while I was visiting my uncle and aunt I met a young man that was a good friend to my cousin. He seemed to have the run of the house because he spent a lot of time there, night and day. My aunt and uncle dearly loved him. He'd walk in open up the pots on the stove to see what was cooking, then turn around and look at me, and my cousin Evelyn and smile, walk out without a word.

I asked my cousin, "Who is *he*, and doesn't he know it is impolite to walk into a room where people are and not speak and open up cooking pots looking into them?"

She just smiled and said, "That's Raymond; he's just like one of the family. He stays out here a lot."

I told her I can't stand him.

She laughed and said, "He don't talk much, but he's ok."

Well, that weekend we went up to the farm in Summit to have a family cookout and of course, Raymond was there. We walked across the field to some peoples house that my uncle knew. As we walked, we had to cross a little spring that had bushes that had to be held back so you could cross the spring. Raymond held the bushes back for everyone until it was my turn to cross. He stood there looking me in the eyes with a funny little grin on his face. Just as I started across he let the bushes go, "whap" and without looking back walked away letting me fend for myself. I was so mad with him; I was fit to be tied!

"I Won't Be Denied"

I said, "You let those bushes come back on me, are you crazy?" He just continued to grin never saying a word.

On the way back I made sure I stayed close to my uncle, but that didn't stop Raymond. He ran ahead holding the bushes back. When uncle and I started across the shallow spring Raymond looked at me with that messy grin, and said, "Want some more?" meaning another whack of the bushes.

I said, "Hell no!" before I knew it and my uncle and Evelyn laughed so hard and so did Raymond. I told him he had to be crazy and for him to stay away from me. He looked at me and shook his head and said, "Uh uh" (meaning no).

I asked my cousin Evelyn, "What's with this guy? I can't stand him"!

She laughed and said, "I think he likes you."

"Not me, girl", I said. The next time I was to go out to uncle and aunt house, I called ahead and asked if Raymond was there and Evelyn said, "No, he hasn't been here in a few days; he works." So, I got my kids together and we went out for homemade ice cream and cake.

We had been there about an hour when I heard Raymond come in. He spoke to my uncle, and then said, "Those are some pretty little girls but whose bigheaded little boy is this?"

Uncle said, "Shut up son, you know who those children belong to."

By then, I had lost it. I said, "They're all mine and if you open your mouth about my son again I will close it pronto."

He just smiled, and said, "I hope so; with a kiss."

I was so stunned until I just stood there glaring at him, wondering what makes this guy tick. He walked into the kitchen and spoke to my aunt, and cousin. My uncle was laughing so hard he was crying. This made me real mad, because Raymond just took a seat and kept looking at me.

The kids liked him instantly, especially Jan she asked him, "Do you have a mother, where do you live, do you go to college like Roy, Jr.?"

He answered all of these questions and said, "Guess what, Janise?"

"What?" her eyes dancing, because she was going to know his secret.

He said very low, "I like your mother."

Jan threw her hands over her mouth and squealed, "Is it a secret?"

He said no and Jan said, "Good, cause I'm going to tell my Mommie anyway", and tell me she did out loud in front of everybody. I didn't know what to say, so I just kept quiet.

When Evelyn and I were cleaning the kitchen up, Raymond said, "Where do you live?"

I turned and looked at him and he said, "I know you live in the projects, but where, what's your address?"

I said, "I don't want any company."

He said, "I'm not company."

When I got ready to go home, my Uncle said, "Raymond, son take Lillian and the children home for me."

I said, "I'll get a jitney to town and catch a bus from there."

Uncle said, "No and Raymond does what I said." Raymond shook his head ok. "Evelyn I'll ride with you all", and that's how he found out where I lived.

The next day he came back to my house. I couldn't believe this guy! He knocked on the door and said, "I came to see you."

I looked at him for a few minutes and then I asked him, "Why?"

He looked straight at me and said, "Because I wanted to."

I said ok, asked him in told him to have a seat.

He said, "I'd like to take you out; will you go?" I thought to myself this guy is persistent. I looked at him and said, "I'll have to see about a baby sitter." Then he said he would pay the sitter.

Well I got the baby sitter and got ready to go out. It proved to be a very nice evening. He seemed to relax with me and began to talk about our getting together. We dated for three months and got married. There were some good times, and some bad times, but we went through them together.

As I write, I'm remembering how hard it must have been for him to become a husband and instant father of four kids, not being able to be footloose and fancy-free anymore.

Instead having to watch every cent in order to stay abreast of everything, I worked and helped make ends meet. We would sit and watch the kids play for hours. Most of the time, we would join in the games with them.

The holidays were always fun, enjoyable times for us. We weren't able to buy ribs to bar-b-que but we would have bar-be-qued neck bones, cole slaw, baked beans, potato salad, kool-aid, and cookies. We had plenty to share and we really enjoyed playing volleyball, hide spy, and hop- scotch. By night, Raymond and I would be real tired, but we didn't let on.

Oh what a joyous time when we got our first car, a 1962 Chevy Station Wagon. By that time, I was working shifts making a good salary. Raymond had come home a few months earlier and told us we were going to move out of the projects to Piney Woods. The kids and I were overjoyed. We all had mixed emotions, hating to leave our project home and all of the precious neighbors we truly loved, from the babies to the elderly, but anxious to begin our lives in our new home. Everything was looking up.

When I'd get on my long weekend I'd go home, wash, iron, and then season chicken to fry, and pack a bag with candy and cokes. When the kids got out of school, I'd let them pop a grocery bag of pop corn, then I'd fry the two chickens I had seasoned. I packed our picnic basket with rolls, chicken, napkins, and forks, let the kids put on their pj's, bring their blankets and pillows and off to the drive-in movies we'd go laughing and talking. We would let them buy their cold drinks at the drive-in movie. It was always a double feature, plus cartoons. Sometimes we would go to Atlanta for the weekend and visit our relatives.

Life was good our kids were happy. When Little Raymond was born, we were overjoyed. My husband and I truly loved each other, but there's always a devil lurking. So, trouble stuck its head up again. Oh well, "I won't be denied." I'm going to continue to pray and *put God first*. He'll fight my battle.

It's hard to love your neighbor share what you have and then find out that she's trying to break up your marriage, but *God is good*, he worked it out for me, and yes, I can truly say that I don't hold a grudge against my ex-neighbor. Today as I sit here writing, I'm smiling and thanking God, because our kids are grown with some grown kids of their own. On May 2nd my husband and I will be married 46 years. Sometimes we sit and talk about things in the past and look toward the future.

Raymond and I were talking about my condition when I said, "I wish the doctor would call and tell me something." I was speaking of the results of my mammogram test biopsy when the phone rang. It was my doctor with the results. When he told me that the results was cancer I had a sinking feeling come over me. I looked up at Raymond and I could see he was getting upset. I knew that would cause him to have a set back, so I asked God to help me be strong and he did.

When Raymond saw me smile and say, "Oh well, I'm no better than nobody else to have it." I know Jesus is a healer and he would bring me through this just as he has so many times before. Our children had prayer with us over the telephone; that lifted our spirits so that I could call the rest of my family.

"Thank you Jesus for being my burden bearer. I'm grateful and I give you all of the praise."

The doctor was very nice. He explained the choices I had. Our daughters (all three of them) listened, asked questions, and thanked him. On the way home, they asked me and Raymond to get a second opinion. So off to Atlanta, Georgia we went. After more tests with three doctors, I found them to be what I needed, and this brings me to today, the day of my surgery.

I'm still calm because I trust my maker to watch over me. My husband, daughters, and sons are kind of nervous but as usual, "I won't be denied" because I know the God I serve is all seeing and all knowing. I've always trusted him and I trust him now. The last thing I remembered before going to sleep (being put under by the anesthesiologist) is saying, "Lord I stretch my hands to thee, and thank you Jesus."

Next thing I knew the nurse was saying, "Wake up Mrs. Lewis; don't you want to go to your room?"

I shook by head yes and kind of drifted off again then felt the sensation of being carried to my room. My husband and daughters were there waiting and smiling; it was wonderful to see them. Oh, what a mighty God we serve! Then I saw my adopted daughter and our play brother. They had driven down to be with us. Again God had blessed me with what he was about, *Love*.

Later that evening, my room was full of my family rejoicing and thanking God for his blessings. The next day our youngest daughter, Patti, came at 9:30 a.m. bathed and dressed me in a beautiful red p.j. outfit. Then in came the nurse saying, "You're discharged, Mrs. Lewis." I was overjoyed. "Thank you Jesus, thank you." I enjoyed most of my family over the weekend.

Monday morning we met my oldest daughter, K.K. at the doctor's office. What a wonderful blessing we received. He said, "Your lymph nodes and tissues were benign. You don't have take chemo, but you'll have to take radiation", and explained everything to us about it. Oh, what a mighty God we serve! I felt like the spirit of the living God had fallen fresh on me. "Lord Jesus, thank you for letting me be able to continue to help where help is needed."

Well, tomorrow is Thursday and my radiation appointment is at 11:00 a.m. I'm looking forward to going home next week. My husband was full of joy every time he came to see me, but when it was time for him to go home, he hated to leave me and I hated to see him go but I knew I had to remain cheerful, so he could leave and go to work in peace. After retiring, he had gotten a job that he enjoyed at Sam's; he got a chance to see a lot of people coming to shop.

We (my husband and I) had been looking forward to the day when my doctors would say I could go home to Chattanooga and it was a joy to hear them finally say I could go. Our daughter and our son-in-law were super good to me. They treated me like a queen. My nieces and nephews were all very loving and kind to me. Our children's friends were encouraging. There's an old saying "out of everything bad something good happens." Even with cancer, so much goodness came to me. All I could say over and over again was "Thank you Jesus, thank you Jesus."

Well, I went to get ready for my radiation everyone was very nice about explaining what to expect during my treatments, which was a blessing. It's only natural to be afraid of the unknown, but they soon put me at ease. Today I got my first radiation treatment. Everything went well. I'm still keeping the faith because Jesus gave his life to save us, and by his stripes I'm healed, thank you Jesus!

This is truly a blessed day for my family and me. I 'm taking my last radiation treatment. As I walk into the building, I look around and speak to the people that are waiting for their turns to receive their treatment and I smile, speak and say a prayer for them in hopes, that all goes well for them too. Everyone is so caring and sharing which makes things easier for you to go through your treatments.

As I lie down on the treatment table, get in position for my last treatment, I look up at the beautiful familiar picture that has been painted on a piece of cloth. It's a scene of a mountain that's snow capped with drizzles of snow draining down the side of the mountain in little patches. Just before you reach the bottom of the mountain there are beautiful flowers all a bloom, green grass that has popped up at the base of the mountain with a small body of water adjacent. At the very top of this beautiful scenery is a beautiful blue sky.

This scenery is so relaxing and it reminds me of how great God is. He is in control of everything in the world, because he made it. There's beautiful soft music that played to soothe you, and the technicians are wonderful. They make sure you are comfortable; they encourage you by answering your questions if you have any. I'm a firm believer that out of everything bad something good happens, because God steps in and soothes the hurts, protects us in a loving and caring way. As the beams enter my body, I lay there praying and thanking God for blessing me with the help I was getting.

Well, my last treatment is over and as I get off of the treatment table, looking around the room that has been my medical haven, I thank God for his many blessings. Even though a portion of my chest, arm, and entire left breast is different, I thought how blessed I am. I'm alive! I'm alive! I can still enjoy my family and friends and help others that need help.

I've just returned from a weekend retreat in the mountains surrounded by a beautiful lake. Oh what a glorious weekend it was. I met so many wonderful people, and we shared our feelings. It was a joy to be relaxed and be able to talk about what was happening to you without having to cover up how you really feel, because you don't want your family worried.

I'm a great lover of my family. I often think of a conversation I had with a young member of my family. She is a lot like me in many ways. I truly love each and every member of my family but she seemed to creep into my heart in a way that took me back to my young years, because she was experiencing some of the same things I had experienced. I think of her often, and want her to know that I care, but most of all, God cares.

Well life goes on and I feel compelled to complete my story, because "I won't be denied." I always look forward to seeing my cousin Beth that lived in Atlanta because she was always full of life and fun. She was a pretty girl and my aunt dressed her real nice.

I remember one special day my aunt sent us to the commissary to get some groceries. We were in a happy mood, and off we went feeling real grown up. It was a wonderful place to shop. There was so much to choose from and of course Beth being Beth after getting what was on the list she got a lot of extra goodies knowing that her mother (my aunt) would only look at her and laughs and say "Girl, you a solid mess."

My aunt could fry chicken like you've never tasted. She had a secret recipe and I watched her very closely so I could try it. I told her about it and she said that's good "Baby Lil, I knew you could do it."

We had a lot of good times together. Even after I got married and had children, she always let us know that we were more than welcome and that she loved us.

Beth took me over to see my great aunt and I met my cousin Judy. She was a hard working attractive young woman with four kids, two boys and two girls. We became very close and it was always a joy to have her come visit us in Chattanooga; we were just as happy to visit with them in Atlanta. It tore my heart in two when God called them home, but I know he knows what's best for us.

Today is Wednesday and it's cowboy movies day and it's hard for my husband Raymond to leave the TV, but he does, because we're driving to Atlanta, Georgia. It's time for me to be checked by the doctors

"I Won't Be Denied"

who attended my surgery and radiation treatment. We're a day early so I can get a good night's rest and not have to rush to get there.

It's a beautiful, sun shiny day, and I drove from Chattanooga to Marietta, Georgia. Raymond drove on into Atlanta because we didn't know the exact place to meet my relative so we went to our favorite hot dog place and called her.

She came to meet us with a beautiful smile and a caring hug. She is an adorable young lady, smart, attractive, firm but fair, loves God, a Christian most of all and it shines through. We can feel the love whenever we're around her. God had blessed her with a wonderful husband and two great boys. We truly love them; they're a joy to be around.

Well it's early Thursday morning and I'm up at 4:35 a.m. writing. Soon I'll shower and dress and my youngest daughter, Patti, and granddaughter Monique will carry me to see my doctors.

Well we stopped by the place where my daughter works and was greeted gleefully. The senior citizens are so sweet it's always good to see them. Uh, oh! Monique is in seventh heaven when she's around them, so she gave us a hug and kiss, and said "See yah", and off we went to see my doctors.

My doctors were really pleased with me. My lab results were great--thank God for the wonderful blessing! I don't have to go back for six months. I just can't stop praising his name he's been so good to me. I have a lot of sick friends and I've lost some by death. Every time I say, "Oh thank you Jesus, you're so good to us even in our trying times." Then I know and say, "It could have been me, but oh Lord you blessed me again, and again by letting me go on a little longer. Thank you, Thank you!"

Well we're back home and I must continue to tell my story, because it may help someone else to keep the faith. I'll be going to have my first mammogram after surgery and radiation on Tuesday. My prayers are that all is well. I have faith in my heavenly Father because he's in control.

My cousin Beth came to visit me Friday of last week and stayed until Thursday of this week. We really enjoyed her and hated to see her leave. I really enjoy TV as most people do. It enables you to see and hear so many things, but I have never seen anyone get into whatever they're looking at like Beth. She doesn't hear anything you say to her. She makes all kinds of faces, she fights and talks, but when she screws her face up, fold her arms and rocks back and forth kicking her feet straight out you'll laugh until you're weak. She hasn't changed at all. She's still full of life and it was a joy to have her here.

Well it's July, hot, rainy, sun shiny which is good for Irvin and Mela's garden. It's a picture to behold; beans, squash, peppers, tomatoes, collard greens, turnip greens, cabbage, bell peppers and their flowers are beautiful. It seems that some people have green thumbs. Today I had another mammogram and all is well--thank God for my blessing!

There are so many things I would like to do to help others. Sometimes it seems that all you do is still not enough. As I look back over my life I can't help but give my savior all of the honor and praise for all of the many things he's brought me through: sickness, heartaches, hunger and lots of danger.

When I was raising my kids, I can remember feeling like I couldn't go any further. Seems like the harder I worked the less I had. I truly loved my kids and wanted the best for them. So I kept going. I got up one morning realizing that my money was very low. My kids needed several things and food was low. I walked down the street to a lady's house that seemed like my mother, and talked with her.

She was very wise and had been through a lot of hardship. As we talked, things began to look brighter and I felt better and vowed that "I wouldn't be denied" because God is in control. I walked back home a few doors away feeling good about myself. I put a pot of grits on to cook, make toast, scrambled some eggs and called my kids downstairs to eat. They came down all happy taking about the great things they were going to do that day. As I poured the last to the milk in their glasses, I said a silent prayer thanking the Lord for letting me be over their lives.

By the time they had finished eating a neighbor knocked on the door asking if I could fix her hair and her little girl's too.

I said, "Yes, as soon as I clean my kitchen up. Have a seat. Would you like a cup of tea?" She said, "No thank you; I just finished breakfast."

"I Won't Be Denied"

After I finished my kitchen I did her hair and she was very pleased and so was I to get the money for fixing her hair. I didn't charge her for fixing her little girl's hair because I knew she was just like me, living in the projects trying to make it. Before I could put my curler and straighten comb up another customer came to get her hair done and before the day was gone, I had fixed four heads and had money to buy more food and milk.

So you see how good God is; he always sends somebody. "Thank you Lord. All we have to do is trust you. You'll make everything all right."

The next day was Sunday and I got my kids ready for Sunday school and church. They were anxious to go so they could see their friends and run up to see their grandmother (their father's mother) after Sunday school for a treat. I stayed home, made up beds, and cleaned the bathrooms laid out play clothes so they wouldn't ruin their good clothes playing. I put dinner on to cook so it would be ready when they got home. I cooked green beans (potatoes on top), corn bread, smothered chicken, icebox pie and made lemonade. I went upstairs and relaxed in a nice bath. I lay across the bed thinking about going to work Monday morning. I got up dressed in a nice cotton dress, a pair of silver mules, combed my hair and felt good about myself.

My kids came in full of news about church and what grandmamma said and almost in the same breath "Mommie, what are we going to do this evening? Are we going to visit our friends or are we going to stay home and play with our friends here and have treats?"

Well I said, "We'll see what we can do later, but we'll have fun together no matter what."

They looked up from their dinner and said, "O.k., Mommie" and I thought to myself how blessed I am to have them. I love them with every fiber of my being.

Well after we finished dinner, Miss Daisy came by to see if my kids could go with her for bible stories and candy. They were overjoyed and wanted to go. I said yes.

As I look back, I can't help but compare the way the housing projects were then and the way they are today. We were so thankful to have a nice place to stay and we worked hard to keep it that way. We planted flowers and kept the inside spotless. Now all you can see is apartments in the projects boarded up and I think to myself, what a waste. There are so many people that would really appreciate a decent place to stay.

It was a joy to walk to the neighborhood store and see all of the beautiful flowers, friendly faces, children playing and just being able to walk without being afraid of being mugged, was truly a blessing.

Today is different; if you walk to the store or just walk any place you have to be very careful. You have to be careful, even in your own house. You have to be sure to lock your doors and make sure everything is secured even when you drive your car. This is too sad.

Time really passes and there are so many things to do. We've had our minds set on buying another house. One that we could finish raising our kids and do all of the family things together in, like big cookouts, breakfasts, and inviting all of our relatives to come and celebrate holidays.

We have looked at several houses, but so far we haven't found one we could afford that would be big enough for our family. So, we're off again today, my friend Vee and I. We decided to turn down East 5th Street, and just before we reached to end of the block, on my left was a "For Sale" sign. We stopped the car and got out to look the house over hoping the door would be open so we could have a look inside, but, of course it was locked. I walked over to the kitchen window and looked in, and really got excited. There were old-fashioned white cabinets that I had always wanted. I looked in the window of the dining room; there were beautiful hardwood floors.

I took the name of the real estate company and the telephone number and rushed to call the number. I was told someone could meet me at three o'clock the next day to show me the house. I was elated and so was Vee! I could hardly sleep that night. I just lay there and prayed.

The next day seem to drag by before it was time to go meet to see the house inside. Finally, we met and as he showed us the house. I prayed "Lord, let this be our house." He showed me the basement.

As we started up the steps, I looked back at him and said, "I sure hope everything goes well." This feels like the place for my family and me.

"I Won't Be Denied"

He answered and said, "Mrs. Lewis, there's always a place for everyone, and this can be the place for you and yours."

Everything went well, and thanks be to God; He blessed us with this house. Now that all paper has been signed and everything has been officially done, we were ready to move in.

We're really excited about moving into our new house! I worked shifts, and it was hard to get off unless it was your off day, even on holidays. So Mommie, Raymond, and the kids did the moving because Raymond was working straight shifts at the time. He got in touch with a friend who had a truck and the moving began. When I got off work that evening, the moving was done and my family was waiting for me so I could see if I was pleased with what had been done.

Talking about being pleased, I was more than pleased. I thanked God for our blessing of a home we could be happy in. We began to plan all of the wonderful things we were going to do. My uncle and aunt came over and they loved the house. Mommie was really happy; she was as busy as a bee making sure everything was intact. Our kids were proud of living in this beautiful house. My grandbabies, K.K.'s daughters, seem to realize we were going to have some good times here. They were two beautiful little girls, full of life, always eager to do fun things. Life was good for a while, then, as life would have it, dark clouds began to roll in.

My great aunt Eliza needs me to come to Athens (GA) to see her. Off we went on my long weekend. I wasn't pleased with her surroundings. There was something going on with her that I couldn't put my finger on. She only talked about family, cooking, and said nothing about her health. When we got ready to leave, she hated to see us leave and asked me to be sure to come back soon. It was something about the way she looked at me that gave me a worried feeling, so I decided to go back on my shift break.

I caught a bus and away I went. She was elated to see me. She was still doing domestic work for the family that she was raised around as a child. She was only able to dust and cook mostly. She was ninety years old, but her memory was really sharp. That first day was lovely; we laughed and talked about the things she did as a child on the plantation. She said,

> "When I was a little girl, I lived on the plantation with my parents. They were slaves at that time, but they belonged to a kind family. Every evening when the mistress would go out to lock the slaves up for the night, she would carry me with her to carry the little basket with the keys in it. As we walked from cabin to cabin, she would bid them goodnight and lock them in. The cabins had a little window that they could look out of and they could close it by pulling it close if the weather was bad or leave it open for fresh air if the weather was hot. During the day, I would have been told by the slave that had been picked to go to the storehouse to get ham, bacon, or whatever they wanted to pass the key so they could get out to do their taking. When the mistress locked them in, I'd give them the key. They'd reach

to the side of the little window, unlock the door very quietly as she moved on the other cabins, and I'd take the key when they'd unlock the door and drop it back in the basket. They never got caught because mistress always slept late and the head house slave would have to get up and unlock the slaves' doors. He knew what was happening so he would act like he was unlocking all of the cabins jut in case someone was watching."

My great aunt would stop talking and look off in space for a while then she would look back at me and laughed that funny little laugh, "hee, hee, hee."

She was very intelligent because she spent most of her life in the big house with the mistress. Her mother was the head cook so that gave her the run of the house with the children of the mistress and master. You would have thought she finished college she was so knowledgeable.

I have a few pictures of my fore parents and they were well dressed, and from the things my great aunt told me, they were well learned too, because after they slipped and learned how to read and write, they read everything they could get their hands on.

They believed in working for what you wanted and going to church. They were all of the Methodist faith and attended faith fully. They were honest, caring, and sharing people who believed in doing unto others, as you would have done unto you. Sometimes I would sit and talk with my great Aunt Eliza for over an hour or until she began to nod, then I would ease out of the room and let her sleep.

She loved it when I'd get her up after her bath, all lotioned, powdered, hair arranged, and dress her in her gown and nice robe. I'd put her in her wheelchair and push her to the breakfast room where she could look out of the window. She always enjoyed a hot cup of tea and I would have one with her. She was something to behold! She had a queenly manner about her; nice manners, and her whole face would light up when she smiled. It was a very sad day when she passed. She looked up at me and said, "You are my darling", and was gone. I'm truly glad that God blessed us with her.

Well life goes on and time brings about a change. My schedule is full and I'm excited about fellowshipping with all of my fraternal members. It's time to go and we've packed the car. As we entered the car, we uttered a prayer for safety going and for our return home.

It was a gloomy day; we ran in and out of showers of rain, then as we traveled down the highway, the sun came from behind the clouds. We talked about the beautiful wildflowers, the cows that roamed the pastures and life in general.

All of the sudden, we had to slow down to almost a stop, there were long rows of cars. Finally, when we reached a certain point there were patrol cars blocking our path with the officers directing us to the exit. We began to run in and out of small towns I never knew existed. We marveled at the beautiful flowers with farms to match--all kinds of beautiful flowers. It was a joy to witness such beauty.

We reached our destination safe and sound, and checked into the motel. As I walked back to our station wagon, I saw some of our members. I waited for them to reach me and I greeted them, "Hi! Gee I'm so glad to see all of you", and they greeted me the same way.

There was a new face among them and I was introduced to a new member, a nice young man. I said, "Welcome; we are elated to have you join our Fraternal Family." It's very important to keep our fraternal bloodline flowing.

It's the first Sunday and I'm off to Church. As I entered the Church, beautiful music reached my ears and I could hardly wait to get to my seat so I could join in the beautiful singing, praying, and praising God for all of his blessings. Communion and fellowshipping was wonderful!

My Daddy is 91 years old and we're really nervous about his driving. My sister called and said my niece told her that Daddy almost hit another car. He drove right over into the lane where the car was. My niece yelled just in time for him to miss hitting the car in the other lane. Now we are trying to figure a way to stop him from driving. He's very strong willed so you have to out smart him. Oh well, where there's a will there's a way. We'll just wait and see how we can pamper him into it.

My, how time flies! My children are teenagers and full of life, interested in baseball, football, band, and school dances. Then came the proms, tuxedos, prom dresses, and the excited chatter of whose taking whom. I often think of the times. I worked sixteen hours or worked a second job to help make ends meet. Then before I could blink my eyes, they are all grown up. Then come the serious dating, engagements, weddings, receptions, and loads of gifts from family and friends and after a while of being married, the blessed event of babies and life goes on and on. Then some of the grand kids are grown and we're now blessed with three little great grandsons. Then I look back over m life and truly say, "Thank you, Lord, I haven't been denied; I've been blessed in a mighty way!"

"I Won't Be Denied"

LILLIAN'S CONVERSATION WITH DADDY

(Lillian) "Daddy, tell me something about your childhood—your parents, sisters and brothers, and other relatives. I met some of them, but not all of them."

(Daddy) "When I was a little boy, I lived and played in the area where your oldest daughter (K.K.) and my granddaughter live now. We went to school in a one-room building. It was so old they stopped us from using it and built a church, where we went to school after they finished church services.

There was a creek nearby, and my family grew corn and wheat near there. After it had grown and my family had picked it, we would all put it in a wagon drawn by a mule to Winn's Mill where the corn and wheat was milled, and made into wheat and flour. We would be happy because there would be good bread for supper, breakfast, and a lot of meals after.

There was a big place by the name of White Water where the rich white folks would go to swim and have fun. No Negroes were allowed except to work and serve them. There were two trains called Little Southern that took you to Fayetteville and Big Southern that took you to Jonesboro. In order to ride you would have to light a piece of paper to flag the trains down. Every time I would hear it coming, I would wait until it got near and I would holler as loud as I could and say "go 'head, go 'head; I'm going to ride you one day." We didn't have anything to ride so we walked no matter how far it was.

I finally got a chance to go to Atlanta to visit my older brothers, Waymond and Oscar, my oldest sister Roxie Jane, and my grandmother. They took me around and showed me the sights and Booker

"I Won't Be Denied"

T. Washington School. I really felt good to see all of this.

My grandmother was truly a praying woman. She prayed day and night. My daddy wanted me to come back home (Fayetteville), but I wouldn't go because I had found me a job in Atlanta at Henderson's Mayonnaise Plant on Whitehall Street, about a block off of McDaniel. I worked on the label machine, and I had to clean and close the place up.

Oh, I forgot to tell you that my daddy finally got a mule of his own and when he ran out of tobacco and had no money, we would gather eggs from the hen house, then ride the mule six or seven miles to trade the eggs for tobacco for daddy.

When I was too small to work in the field, my brothers, sister, and cousins, would go to a place called Hops Crossing to work and make extra money for the family and, of course, they would carry me with them so they could look after me while they worked. They would carry an old quilt and lay me on it when I got tired of watching them work.

One day, they forgot and left me there asleep and when they got home, they missed me and had to go back to Hops Crossing in the dark looking for me and found me still asleep on the quilt where they put me. They were happy to find o.k and me still asleep. I would have had a fit if I had woke up and seen them gone.

My daddy went to stay with his grandparents when he was young. His real name was James Hollins, but they changed it to James Keith, after them. My mother's name was Rachel Keith. My mother passed at 35 years old and left eight kids.

"I Won't Be Denied"

My daddy married a nice lady named Beulah Frost. She had two sisters named Dora and Vera Frost and a brother named Jim Frost. Ms. Beulah was always cooking something good to eat but Sundays were special. She would bake a big pound cake and open up some good peaches she canned in the summer. We would parch peanuts and play a game called Jack in the Bush. I don't remember how the game goes, but it was fun.

One day we were all playing in the back yard and my brother Oscar was trying to show us how brave he was by putting his hand on the chopping block and said "cut these old fingers off; I don't need them" and one of my cousins did just that. Boy, when we saw the blood and his fingers gone, we all had a fit. My bother took off running and hollering toward the house and we scattered in different directions. We so scared we couldn't talk. Of course, we were punished, and my bother healed without three of his fingers."

(Lillian) "Gee daddy, you guys were really something, but God really took care of all of you in the good, bad, and fun times. That just goes to show you that he is real and the same yesterday, today, and forever. Praise His Holy Name!"

ACKNOWLEDGEMENTS

To Raymond, my husband, who is my strength. In memory of my mother, Mrs. Fannie Mae Keith, who taught me to pray and believe in God. My uncle Roy Keith Sr. who always taught us it was someone else in the world besides us. To my children Karen, Janise, Patti, William, and Raymond Jr. and last but not least, Mr. Ernest Hamilton who encouraged me to write this book in hopes that it will help someone else.

ABOUT THE AUTHOR

Lillian K. Lewis is a strong Christian woman who believes in sharing with those who are less fortunate. Lillian strongly encourages our youth to excel while praising the elderly, valuing their knowledge and daily guidance. She resides in Tennessee with husband Raymond where they raised three daughters and two sons.

Printed in the United States
26645LVS00001B/208-309